EUGÉNIE ROCHEROLLE
TOUCH OF BLUE

OFFICIAL FEDERATION CHOICE
National Federation of Music Clubs
Junior Festivals

Dedicated to Alex Bloom, Krista Bruce Easton, Laryssa Lambros, Kate Holman,
Neesha Ramchandani, Paige Rossetti, and Chrissy Franks Woods

CONTENTS

Editor: JAMES L. KING III
Production Coordinator: KARL BORK
Art Design: MICHAEL RAMSAY

THE BLUES

The blues has a special place in American music, an important place. With vocal origins in black American folk music, the melancholy nature of the blues is characterized by use of a flat 3rd, 7th, and sometimes 5th degree of the scale. These flatted notes are known as "blue notes."

Related to (but separate from) jazz, the blues was first popularized by W. C. Handy, a black musician who published "Memphis Blues" in 1912 and later "St. Louis Blues." By the 1920s, the first blues recordings were made of the Mississippi delta "country" traditions and other southern regional variants.

With the migration north to Chicago, the blues developed into a coarser, more urban sound, and by the late 1940s had led to the style known as rhythm and blues. By then, amplification of the instruments had become standard.

The blues has had a decisive influence on Western popular music, adopted and imitated in every venue, including that of Broadway song literature. It has influenced rock 'n' roll music and continues as an independent genre, with the improvisatory tradition of the blues still a vital feature.

Eugénie Rocherolle

LATE TRAIN

EUGÉNIE ROCHEROLLE

Moderately slow (♩ = 96)

REMEMBERING YOU

EUGÉNIE ROCHEROLLE

THINKING BLUE

EUGÉNIE ROCHEROLLE

Tempo primo

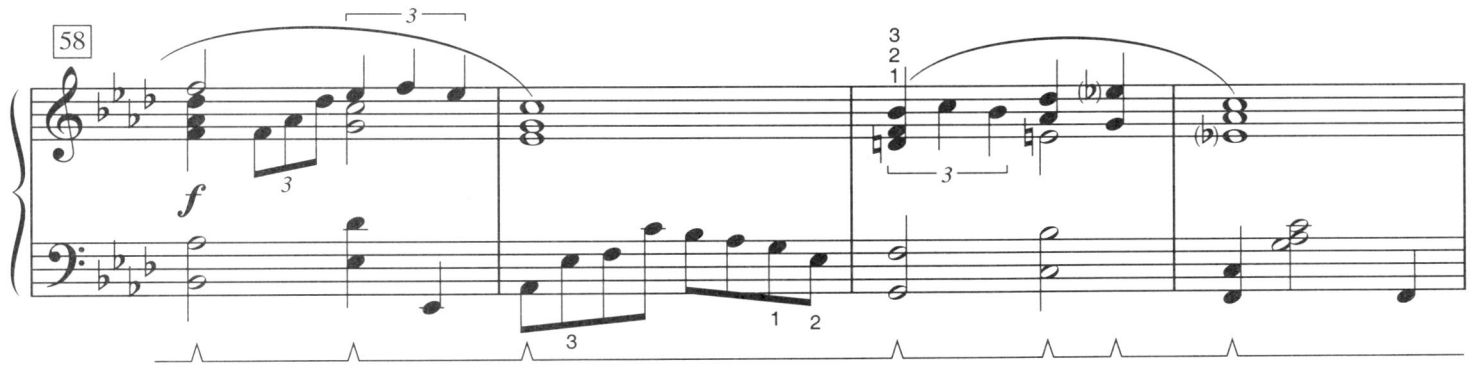

*Smaller hands may omit the lower octave in measures 57 and 58.

ELM00023A

WALKIN' HOME

EUGÉNIE ROCHEROLLE

13

ELM00023A

14

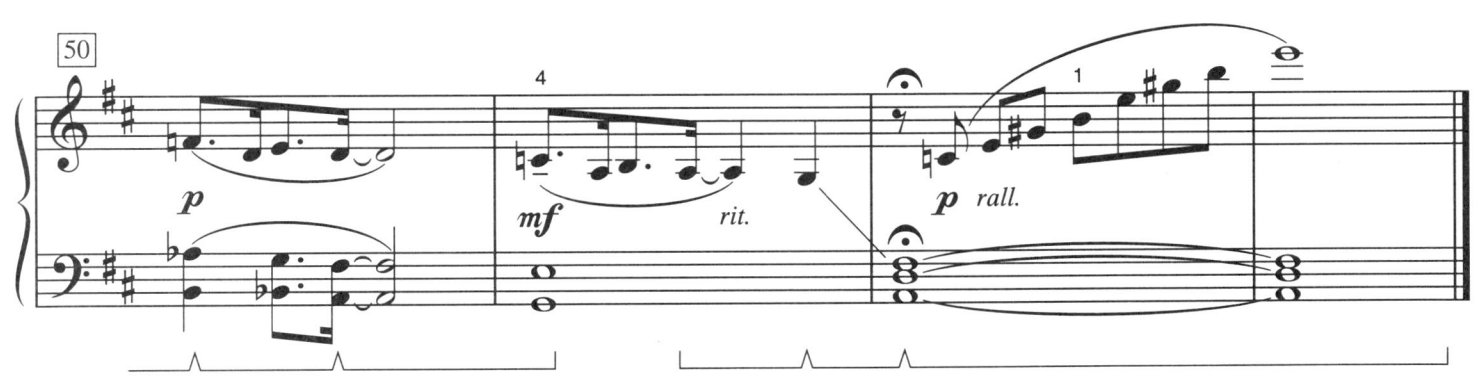

EASY STREET

EUGÉNIE ROCHEROLLE

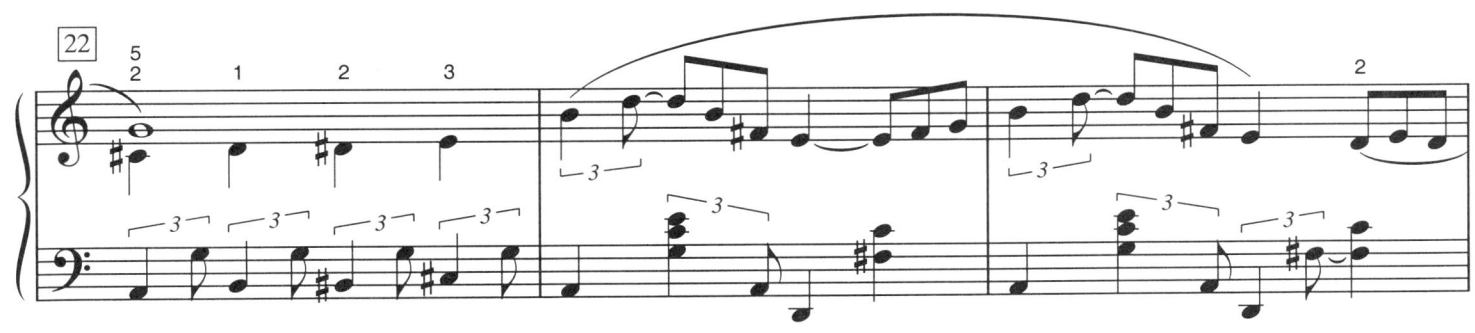

LONELY NIGHTS

EUGÉNIE ROCHEROLLE

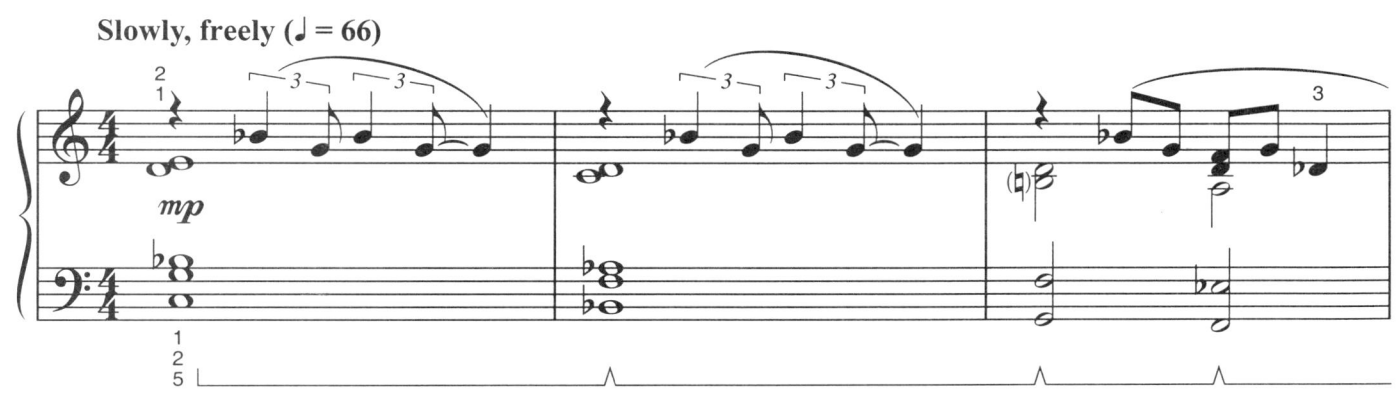

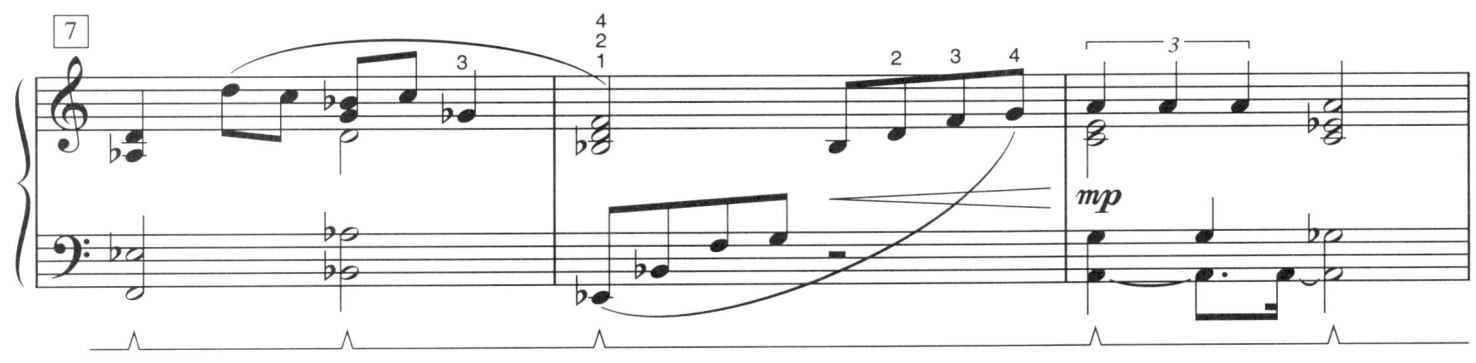

ELM00023A

20

*Bass clef D may be played with the right hand.

FEELING MISTY

Eugénie Rocherolle

ELM00023A

24